Career Discovery

Careers If You Like Helping People

Gail Snyder

ReferencePoint Press®

San Diego, CA

ReferencePoint
Press®

Picture Credits
Cover: iStockphoto/Kali9
 8: iStockphoto/Monkey Business Images
42: iStockphoto/Fat Camera
49: iStockphoto/LisaFx

© 2018 ReferencePoint Press, Inc.
Printed in the United States

For more information, contact:
ReferencePoint Press, Inc.
PO Box 27779
San Diego, CA 92198
www.ReferencePointPress.com

LIBRARY OF CONGRESS CATALOGING-IN-PUBLICATION DATA

Name: Snyder, Gail, author.
Title: Careers If You Like Helping People/by Gail Snyder.
Description: San Diego, CA: ReferencePoint Press, Inc., 2018. | Series: Career Discovery |
   Includes bibliographical references and index. | Identifiers: LCCN 2017004101 (print) | LCCN
   2017012110 (ebook) | ISBN 9781682821374 (eBook) | ISBN 9781682821367 (hardback)
Subjects: LCSH: Social service—Vocational guidance—United States—Juvenile literature. |
   Human services—Vocational guidance—United States—Juvenile literature. | Medical care—
   Vocational guidance—United States—Juvenile literature.
Classification: LCC HV10.5 (ebook) | LCC HV10.5 .S596 2018 (print) | DDC 361.0023/73--dc23
LC record available at https://lccn.loc.gov/2017004101

CONTENTS

Introduction: Making a Difference

Being employed has many satisfactions, not least of which is receiving a paycheck. But for some people—and you may be among them—a good salary is not nearly as important as doing work that helps make other people's lives better. Careers in the helping professions—such as those found in social work, teaching, medicine, and emergency response—come with that important bonus. In addition to a paycheck, people in the helping professions can clearly see the impact of their work on the individuals they serve.

For example, many nurses feel they have done important work when the patients they treat leave their care free of the infections that made them ill. Exhausted firefighters may feel fulfilled when their actions save a life or a family's home. Special education teachers feel proud when their students acquire new skills because of their instruction, and adult literacy teachers experience genuine thrills when the students they have been working with are able to read without hesitation. Says Fran Pellmar, an adult literacy teacher from Edison, New Jersey, "I've always felt that life has to have meaning, and we only go through this route once. And I want my life to make some kind of small difference."[1]

Finding Meaning

In 2007 the University of Chicago issued a report that examined the relationship between career choice and happiness. The survey queried more than twenty-seven thousand American workers on matters relating to their work satisfaction and happiness. Randomly conducted interviews revealed three professions with the highest satisfaction levels: clergy, firefighter, and physical therapist, all helping professions. Some 87 percent of clergy members surveyed expressed great satisfaction with their jobs, while 80 percent of firefighters and 78 percent of physical therapists expressed the same sentiments. "The most satisfying jobs are mostly . . . those involving caring for, teaching and protecting others,"[2] says Tom W. Smith, a spokesperson for the National Opinion Research Center at the University of Chicago.

Those who find meaning in their employment are sometimes called givers, and it seems logical that such people will be more satisfied with their work. Indeed, in a 2014 article for the magazine *Fast Company*, Jessica Amortegui wrote, "Meaning comes when we realize the impact of our work on others. In fact, what distinguishes the most successful givers—versus those who burn out—is not what or how much they give. It is that they know the difference they make on others. People aren't inspired solely by what they do. People are lit up when they know why what they do matters."[3]

Helping the Vulnerable

A career in one of the helping professions can be a good match for people who are compassionate and empathetic. If you have a soft spot for underdogs in movies, books, sports, or real life, you may find your calling in a career that focuses on helping vulnerable members of society. For instance, you might work as a nurse-midwife to help expectant mothers have healthy pregnancies and deliveries. As a social worker, you may be the safety net on which dependent children rely when their parents are unable to maintain safe homes for them. In your role as a firefighter or police officer, you might be the authority figure who responds to an accident, medical emergency, crime, or domestic violence incident. As a nursing home aide, home health aide, gerontologist, physical therapist, or clergy member, you may play an essential role in meeting the needs of frail, poor, or mentally incapacitated elderly people who can no longer care for themselves.

So how can you decide if a career in a helping field is what you truly want? The best way is to volunteer, or if you are old enough and have the time, find a part-time job working with the population you are interested in serving. If you think you might like to work with the elderly, you can volunteer to play board games with local nursing home residents or apply for a job as a meal server. If you are thinking about a career as a professional firefighter, you might volunteer at your local firehouse. Or if there is an Explorer program available in your community—an activity sponsored by the Boy Scouts of America that helps young men and women choose careers—you may consider joining it and volunteering your time in a helping profession.

You might also arrange to shadow an adult in the profession you are considering. Doing so is an excellent way to see how that person spends his or her days. If they really like what they do, adults are often eager to encourage others to enter their profession. They may believe what nineteenth-century poet Ralph Waldo Emerson said about one's life purpose—and you may believe it too. "The purpose of life is not to be happy," he said. "It is to be useful, to be honorable, to be compassionate, to have it make some difference that you have lived and lived well."[4]

Addiction Counselor

A Few Facts

Number of Jobs
About 94,900 as of 2014

Pay
$39,980, average salary in 2015

Educational Requirements
Bachelor's degree

Work Settings
Indoors—in mental health clinics, schools, and prisons

Unemployment Rate
3.3 percent

Future Job Outlook
22 percent growth, much faster than average

Facilitating Recovery

Addiction counselors help individuals and their families who want to put dangerous habits behind them. They may also be professionally known as chemical dependency, substance abuse, or behavior disorder counselors. Whatever title they go by, they typically work with clients who are dependent on dangerous legal or illegal drugs such as tobacco, alcohol, prescription painkillers, heroin, or cocaine. Other addiction counselors work with clients who suffer from an eating disorder or have a gambling problem severe enough to affect their quality of life.

Some addiction counselors are drawn to the field because they have personally struggled with addictions of their own. One such counselor is Donna Mae Depola. She is a credentialed alcohol and substance abuse counselor who was once addicted to cocaine. Depola began using drugs when she was only nine and continued until she was thirty-five. She underwent multiple addiction treatment interventions before becoming drug free. Now she finds that helping others in similar situations is very satisfying.

A counselor takes notes as she listens to a young woman describe her addiction. Addiction counselors help people overcome their insatiable need for drugs, gambling, and other activities that may harm their quality of life.

"There are so many miracles in this field," says Depola. "I try and concentrate on the successes we see and hope that the clients that are still using will come back and get help before it's too late." Depola once worked with a woman who had six children but lost them to the foster care system because she was addicted to drugs. "It took her four years to get clean but when she did she got her children back, graduated college, and now works in the [addiction counseling] field,"[5] says Depola.

Although it is challenging work, the job of addiction counselor receives high marks from U.S. News, an information company that ranks occupations according to variables such as median salary, employment rates, job prospects, stress levels, and work-life balance. U.S. News puts addiction counselor first among all social service jobs, which include occupations such as school psychologist, marriage and family therapist, lawyer, and social worker. In addition, U.S. News ranks addiction counselor fifty-first on its list of the one hundred best jobs. Says addiction counselor Stephen Gumbley, director of the New England Addiction Technology Transfer Center, "I love this work. To see folks grab onto hope and begin to get their lives more orderly is phenomenal."[6]

What Addiction Counselors Do

Addiction counselors cannot solve all of their clients' problems. What they can do, however, is work with clients to help them develop the skills they need to solve their own problems. Oftentimes, addiction counselors work with clients who have multiple issues, which makes finding solutions for them complex. They may need to refer their clients to multiple agencies that can help them with a variety of tasks, such as finding health insurance, signing up for welfare benefits to pay for living expenses, or accessing their local food bank.

Counselors may work with individuals or groups of clients who share similar problems. They are responsible for evaluating their clients' needs and readiness for treatment, developing treatment plans, and teaching them better ways to cope with their daily stresses and unhealthy desires. Addiction counselors may also work with the community at large, such as young students, to discourage them from developing habits that might lead to addiction.

Addiction counselors may also work with other professionals. These may include supervisors who oversee the organizations where they work, as well as individual specialists such as psychiatrists, social workers, and physicians who may have referred their patients to addiction counseling.

What Skills Do You Need?

You may already have some of the skills or traits you need to be an addiction counselor. For example, if you have a desire to help people who have problems, relate well to others, have patience,

It's OK to Be the Bad Guy

"I really wanted to be the favorite counselor. I wanted to be liked. I wanted to be cool. I wanted to be the counselor everyone wanted. In order to obtain this goal, I made special exceptions for clients, ignored their non-compliance, did not always back up my co-workers, developed inappropriately friendly and casual [relationships] with clients, and devalued program rules. It goes without saying that this did not serve my clients, and ultimately did not serve me. I had to come to grips with not always being liked. I had to be okay with being the bad guy."

—Heidi Voet Smith, addiction counselor

Heidi Voet Smith, "Confessions of an Addiction Counselor," *Addiction Professional*, October 30, 2014. www.addictionpro.com.

and are a good listener and communicator, you already have many of the skills that are valued in the field of addiction counseling.

While caring about other people's problems is important, addiction counselors must also keep a professional distance from their clients. In such work, there is a danger that a client could become too dependent on a counselor. In other words, the client may misinterpret the counselor's advice and intentions and develop a friendship or affection for the counselor. Experts in addiction counseling warn that this type of response to a counselor's help can be very damaging to the client. Rita Sommers-Flanagan and John Sommers-Flanagan, professors of mental health counseling at the University of Montana, explain:

This urge for closeness with one's counselor—whether driven by unconscious needs and fantasies, or a more conscious response to being listened to and cared for—is a vulnerable emotional reaction to the helping process. In response to this vulnerability, the ethical professional must find wise and gentle ways to explain these necessary professional boundaries so that clients do not feel embarrassed, judged, or rejected.[7]

In other words, while it is important for the client to trust the counselor, it is the counselor's responsibility to make it clear that the client is expected to eventually leave counseling and get on with life on his or her own.

Some people who enter the field do so because they have experienced addiction issues themselves or indirectly through friends and relatives. However, having that sort of intimate knowledge of addiction is not necessary. As Depola observes, "Just because you lived it doesn't mean you have what it takes to be a counselor. It takes education, dedication and empathy to help others. Every drug is different, every experience is different, and every individual is different. So many people going into the field think because they were addicted that the person has to get recovery like they did."[8]

Where Do Addiction Counselors Work?

Addiction counselors may work in a variety of settings, depending on which population they serve. For example, some work for mental health centers, hospitals, prisons, halfway houses, government agencies, and for-profit institutions. According to the Bureau of Labor Statistics (BLS), the biggest employer of addiction counselors is outpatient care centers. They account for 22 percent of all jobs in the field.

Outpatient centers are community-based facilities that treat clients who live at home but come into the center one or more times a week for counseling sessions. According to Gumbley, addiction counselors who are employed at outpatient facilities work daytime hours, typically 9:00 a.m. to 5:00 p.m. A supervisor determines the number of cases assigned to each counselor. During a typical week in an outpatient center, an addiction counselor meets with clients for about forty-five minutes per session.

Many addiction counselors also work at residential treatment centers, also known as inpatient treatment centers. According to the BLS, 20 percent of addiction counseling jobs are found at residential treatment centers. A residential facility serves clients whose addictions to drugs or alcohol are so severe that they must be under twenty-four-hour watch. Typically, residential centers are high-security facilities enclosed in fences and policed by guards. Sometimes clients are ordered by courts to remain in inpatient facilities until they can be trusted to live in the community. Because inpatient facilities serve patients in residence, addiction counselors must be prepared to work shifts that are outside normal daytime work hours.

According to the BLS, another 14 percent of addiction counselors work with individuals and families who are coping with substance abuse. Many of these counselors are employed in private practices—they either maintain offices where they see their clients or go to their clients' homes. Another 11 percent of addiction counselors are employed by hospitals, while 10 percent work for state and local government agencies. These counselors usually address substance abuse problems among people who are unable to afford private addiction counseling.

What Training Do You Need?

A bachelor's degree in addiction studies is usually all that is needed to become an addiction counselor. There are some exceptions, though. For example, if you wish to work in private practice, where you see patients without being supervised by another person or organization, you may need to get a master's degree.

Moreover, states typically require addiction counselors to meet licensing requirements. To satisfy such requirements, more than sixty thousand counselors in America and other countries have earned the National Certified Counselor designation. By achieving additional requirements, counselors can obtain the Master Addictions Counselor designation. This requires them to have devoted twelve hours of study to addiction during their master's programs or put in five hundred continuing education hours in the field.

Typical Salaries, Growing Demand

According to the BLS, addiction counselors who earn the highest salaries work for government agencies; their salaries averaged $45,140 in 2015. Meanwhile, addiction counselors who worked in hospitals averaged $35,290 in 2015, while counselors who worked in outpatient care centers earned an average of $39,460. Counselors who worked in residential facilities earned $36,100.

Jobs for addiction counselors are growing at a rate of 22 percent per year, which is much faster than average. Two factors are driving that growth. One is that insurance companies are now willing to pay for mental health services, and treatment for addiction falls under that category. The second factor is that the judicial system is changing the way it views and handles drug offenders. Instead of giving significant jail time to drug abusers, courts have come to believe it is better to provide users with effective treatments that give them opportunities to become productive

Seeking the Root Problem

"Too often counselors manage clients based upon their addictive behavior rather than seeing the deficits that drive the behavior. I usually look at the disorder as a symptom; most individuals who are dependent upon substances are self-medicating in response to a root problem (such as sexual abuse, loss or trauma, low self-esteem, loneliness, depression, underdeveloped identity, etc.). I have formed rewarding counseling relationships with many amazing clients as they bravely step away from their destructive coping mechanism. Seeing their courage on the journey to substance-free lives has made me a grateful witness."

—Douglas Klier, addiction counselor

Douglas Klier, "A Day in the Life of a Substance Abuse Counselor," Assumption College, 2016. http://cce.assumption.edu.

citizens. This attitude recognizes that addicted people have the potential to rehabilitate themselves. It is also much cheaper to treat a drug abuser in an outpatient facility than it is to send that person to jail—which typically costs $31,000 a year, according to a 2012 study by the Vera Institute of Justice, a New York City advocacy group.

Once you are a counselor, there may be some opportunities for advancement. Addiction counselors who continue in the profession may become lead counselors who supervise others, or they may become the director of an entire program. As a supervisor or director of an addiction program, you might still see clients but would also be responsible for administrative duties. Such duties might include contacting other social agencies, completing patient charts, and dealing with insurance companies, phone calls, and e-mails.

For the right individual, being an addiction counselor can be highly satisfying. However, counselors must be able to accept that some clients will relapse; some may even overdose and die. On the other hand, many others will go on to lead normal, fulfilling lives no longer marred by addiction. Addiction counselors will take great satisfaction in knowing that their services can be life changing for individuals and their families.

Find Out More

Addiction Technology Transfer Center Network (ATTC)
website: www.attcnetwork.org

The ATTC serves as a national resource for addiction treatment professionals who want to pool their knowledge about the most effective treatment and prevention techniques. The organization consists of ten regional centers, four national focus area centers, and a national coordinating office. Its website offers free online courses on addiction-related topics, a searchable database of intervention and treatment strategies, and links to offices around the country.

American Counseling Association

6101 Stevenson Ave., Suite 600
Alexandria, VA 22304
website: www.counseling.org

The American Counseling Association represents the interests of fifty-six thousand members who are professional counselors. The website contains a short video for students about the profession, has a section of frequently asked questions, and provides some access to articles in the association's monthly journal, *Counseling Today*.

NAADAC, The Association for Addiction Professionals

4 Canal Center Plaza, Suite 301
Alexandria, VA 22314
website: www.naadac.org

NAADAC, The Association for Addiction Professionals, represents the professional interests of eighty-five thousand US and Canadian addiction counselors and related professionals. It provides education, clinical training, and certification services. The website offers access to membership and salary surveys of its members.

Substance Abuse and Mental Health Services Administration (SAMHSA)

5600 Fishers Ln.
Rockville, MD 20857
website: www.samhsa.gov

An agency within the US Department of Health and Human Services, SAMHSA is charged with reducing the impact of substance abuse and mental illness on communities. The SAMHSA website has information on the prevention and treatment of substance abuse, including alcohol, tobacco, marijuana, opioids, and other drugs.

Adult Literacy Teacher

A Few Facts

Number of Jobs

About 77,500 as of 2014

Pay

$50,280, average salary in 2015

Educational Requirements

Bachelor's degree

Work Settings

Community colleges, schools, community organizations

Future Job Outlook

7 percent, about average

Reaching Those Who Want to Learn

Adult literacy teachers work with adults who lack basic reading skills. Their students may be immigrants who want to develop their English language skills so they can find a better job or assimilate into American society. Some students may be American citizens who went through school but failed to develop minimal reading, writing, and math skills. Or they may have dropped out of high school before earning their diplomas and now, as adults, struggle with tasks that require them to read, write, or use numbers. However, all adult literacy students share a common trait: They all want to better their lives.

Adult literacy teachers work with individuals or groups to help them learn skills that can dramatically change their lives, which trickles into the lives of other family members. Monica Brown, who teaches English to immigrants, shares the thrill she received from working with a particularly motivated adult student. Says Brown, "The first time I heard my student, Jose, thank me because he was able to help his mother translate one of her conversations over the phone, I felt so proud to have indirectly helped another family member."[9]

Indeed, when one adult masters literacy skills, the effects can ripple through an entire family. Parents can do a better job of helping their children with their homework. In doing so, they take steps to end the cycle of poverty and incarceration that plagues some families from generation to generation. Perhaps that is why a 2015 survey conducted by the career education website O*NET OnLine found that 67 percent of adult literacy teachers expressed satisfaction with their careers. About 72 percent said their job helps them make the world a better place.

What Do Adult Literacy Teachers Do?

Adult literacy teachers perform their jobs in different ways, depending on whom, where, and what they are teaching. That being said, there are some similarities. All adult literacy teachers create lesson plans that accommodate their students' needs. They teach those lessons, keep tabs on their students' progress by giving tests, help students learn how to study if they lack good study skills, and help students find the resources they need to make the most progress.

If you are interested in the field of adult literacy, there are three areas in which you might work. These include adult basic education, high school equivalency, and English as a second language (ESL). Adult basic education teachers work with adults who want to improve their math and English skills. These students typically read on an eighth-grade level or lower. They recognize that to get a better job they need to acquire new skills. In some cases their lack of such skills prevents them from finding a job that pays enough to allow them to support themselves and their families.

Literacy programs can also help people avoid going back to prison or have a better life after they are released from prison. Deborah Rei teaches classes at a state prison in California. The inmates she works with often have poor literacy skills, in addition to learning disabilities and psychological problems. She explains,

"It is a known fact that recidivism or the rate of return to prison is reduced by 25 to 30 percent when inmates complete academic education programs."[10]

High school equivalency classes are offered to students who want to earn a General Education Development, or GED, diploma. The GED is regarded as the equivalent of the diploma that American high schools award students. Those who want to earn a GED must pass an exam that takes seven and a half hours to complete. The GED test is offered online by state governments and is divided into sections on reading, writing, social studies, and math. To pass, students must score at least 145 points on each section (out of a maximum of 200 points). Most students find that to pass the GED test, they first need to attend classes taught by high school equivalency diploma teachers.

ESL teachers work with adults who have good communication skills in languages other than English. Often new to the United States, these students need to be able to read and speak English to earn a living, attend college or trade school, help their children with homework, or pass the American citizenship test.

What Qualities Do You Need?

Teaching adults who likely come from a different background than your own takes some special characteristics. Certainly, all teachers need to be good communicators, both orally and in writing. In addition, you will need to be patient because adult students may get frustrated more easily than younger ones, and they may be harder on themselves, too. You must therefore be able to motivate people when they are experiencing self-doubt. One way to do that is to focus their attention on the goals you create together and point out incremental steps they have made toward reaching them. If they come from another culture, you must also be willing to learn about that culture so as to honor their heritage, make stronger connections with them, and avoid making gaffes due to cultural differences.

Adult literacy teachers also need to be highly adaptable because students will have very different needs, backgrounds, and skill sets. You must be able to decide the best way to reach each student and also be able to respond to the problems that are likely to arise on the way to meeting that student's goals.

Where Do Adult Literacy Teachers Work?

Adult literacy teachers work in several types of locations. About 29 percent of such teachers work for public or private schools, while nearly as many—about 28 percent—find employment at junior colleges. According to the Bureau of Labor Statistics (BLS), about 7 percent work for health care or social assistance agencies, and another 4 percent find employment with colleges and vocational schools.

Many adult literacy teachers do not typically find day-shift jobs that take place between 9:00 a.m. and 5:00 p.m. That's because most adult learners are working people who can only take classes when they are not working their own jobs. Classes are therefore usually taught early in the morning before the students head off to work or in the evenings after their workdays are done. Moreover, according to the BLS, many adult literacy teachers do not have full-time jobs. Rather, many work part-time or hold a number of part-time positions, enabling them to put together the equivalent of a full-time work schedule.

However, many ESL teachers find full-time employment opportunities in other countries, particularly at universities where students hope to go on to achieve graduate degrees at American colleges. Therefore, many foreign universities recruit ESL teachers. This could be interesting to you if you want to travel after completing your own education.

How Do You Become an Adult Literacy Teacher?

Perhaps you like to read, enjoy writing, are good at math, and want to teach other people those subjects. Those skills are important, but not enough for you to find your place in this field. You will also need the right education, which includes having a bachelor's degree that may be in English or math, as well as a teaching certificate. You must also meet the teaching requirements set by the state in which you intend to work.

It is also possible to earn a master's degree in adult education, either online or in university classrooms. Courses cover topics such as teaching adult learners, lesson planning for adult learners, adult literacy, education learning theories, student assessment practices, and more. Those who have a master's degree in adult education can move into other fields besides adult literacy

A Challenging Profession

"Unlike children, adult learners tend to be very self-conscious, particularly about the way they speak and their pronunciation. They also tend to get frustrated more easily. They get discouraged if they think they've made little to no progress, especially advanced students who may feel they've reached a language plateau beyond which they can't progress. Finally, they are also very hard on themselves, sometimes, demanding unrealistic things like perfect pronunciation or listening."

—Claudia Pesce, adult literacy teacher

Claudia Pesce, "Teaching Adults How-To: Advantages and Challenges," Busy Teacher, 2017. http://busyteacher.org.

and GED instruction. For example, they could become corporate trainers and/or training and development managers who work within a corporation.

It is not necessary for ESL teachers to speak the languages their students speak. For starters, their students will likely speak a variety of native languages—Spanish, Chinese, Korean, and so on—so it is unlikely that any ESL teacher would be fluent in the languages of every student in a class. Also, most students begin their instruction with at least some knowledge of English, so teachers are likely to be able to communicate with them at least a little bit. Finally, most ESL classes emphasize the importance of conducting the lessons entirely in English, thereby challenging students to improve their skills as the class progresses.

Earnings and Future Job Growth

Adult literacy and high school equivalency diploma teachers made an average of $50,280 in 2015, according to figures kept by the BLS. The government agency reports that the highest 10 percent of people in the profession earned more than $83,140, while the lowest 10 percent brought home less than $28,870. The wide spread in salaries is perhaps the result of many teachers' inability to secure full-time work. Teachers who work for public and private elementary and secondary schools earned the highest wages.

The profession is expected to add 5,500 jobs between 2014 and 2024; this represents average growth, according to the BLS. However, with the United States experiencing rising immigration rates, the continued need for ESL teachers seems ensured. Moreover, a 2013 study by the US Department of Education concluded that adult illiteracy remains a significant problem in American society. The study found that the illiteracy rate among American adults remained unchanged in the ten years prior to the study: Some 32 million Americans—or about 14 percent of the American population—lack basic reading skills.

These statistics suggest that there will continue to be a job market for teachers willing to work with adults who lack basic reading, writing, and mathematics skills. If you are a patient person who does not get easily frustrated, enjoys teaching new skills, or finds the prospect of teaching students from other countries and cultures fascinating, than adult literacy teacher belongs on your list of careers to consider.

Find Out More

America's Literacy Directory
website: https://learner.lincs.ed.gov

America's Literacy Directory, part of the Literary Information and Communication System, is a professional learning platform for adult educators funded by the US Department of Education. Type in your zip code to find programs near you that may need volunteers.

Busy Teacher
Elegant E-Learning, Inc.
1466 Limeridge Rd. E.
Hamilton, ON, Canada L8W3J9
website: http://busyteacher.org

Busy Teacher offers free online articles for people who teach English, including stories about teaching English as a second language. There are also worksheets and lesson plans available for browsing.

International Literacy Association
PO Box 8139
Newark, DE 19714
website: www.literacyworldwide.org

The International Literacy Association is a global organization that advocates for literacy. Its research efforts and publications help literacy professionals obtain the latest resources. Visitors to the website can read sample articles from the organization's magazine, *Literacy Today*.

TESOL International Association

1925 Ballenger Ave., Suite 550
Alexandria, VA 22314
website: http://tesol.org

TESOL is an international association of people committed to advancing the English language. The organization has a membership level for college students. It also organizes conventions, publishes a blog and monthly newsletter that are accessible online, and offers an online career center that posts job listings.

Firefighter

More than Putting Out Fires

Television shows such as *Chicago Fire* or *Rescue Me* show just a small part of what being a professional firefighter is all about. There is no question the job involves fighting fire. Who hasn't seen a fire engine racing through city streets, siren blaring, on its way to a blaze? Firefighters often scale tall ladders to attack blazes that have erupted in buildings several stories high. Some even jump out of airplanes or travel by helicopter to tackle wildfires in remote locations.

But there is much more to being a firefighter than putting out fires. According to the National Fire Protection Association, a trade group based in Quincy, Massachusetts, two out of three phone calls received by fire departments across the country do not involve fires. For example, many people who call are suffering medical emergencies; some firefighters have found themselves delivering babies when expectant mothers are unable to get to hospitals. This illustrates how firefighters are first responders in the truest sense of the word—their job is to help people who find themselves in all kinds of perilous situations.

For example, firefighters are typically summoned to the scenes of automobile accidents. They may need to cut drivers or passengers out of crushed vehicles using a tool known as the Jaws of Life or otherwise help those in need. Russell Whaley, a firefighter from Chandler, Arizona, responded to a car accident in 2015. When Whaley and his coworkers arrived at the scene, they found a mother, a baby girl, and a four-year-old boy named Lucas in need of assistance. While the other emergency professionals provided medical care to the baby and mother, Whaley helped keep Lucas calm and focused on something other than the accident. He sat on the ground and read the boy a children's book. Even though he did nothing that day that involved fire, Whaley's work was tremendously important. Says Whaley, "It reinforces what I was taught at the academy, and that is every day I come to work we make a difference in someone's life in a positive way; for me, that day it was sitting down and reading a book."[11]

Where Firefighters Work

If you enjoy working indoors and outdoors, being a firefighter will allow you to do both. Professional firefighters spend a lot of time at the firehouse waiting for emergency calls to come in. But when they're out on those calls, firefighters may find themselves inside burning buildings, up on rooftops, or inside other people's homes, responding to medical emergencies. Firefighters who respond to wildfires may spend several days outdoors working to halt the spread of blazes that span dozens or even hundreds of miles and have the potential to destroy people's homes or valuable natural space.

Most professional firefighters work for city governments. According to the Bureau of Labor Statistics (BLS), 91 percent of firefighters work for such local authorities. Others find jobs with federal and state government agencies, among them the US Forest Service, the National Park Service, and the Bureau of Indian Affairs. Also, some firefighters work at airports, where they may need to respond to emergencies involving commercial airplanes.

Experiencing Life and Death on a Daily Basis

"Being a firefighter has got to be the greatest job there is. Being able to help people. When you see people at their best, you rejoice. You have those times when you are a part of bringing a new life into the world. And then you go to situations when the news is not so good and people die. You are able to lend some comfort to families, let them know that everything was done to help their loved one."

—Ty Silcox, fire chief

Quoted in Teresa Stepzinski, "Orange Park Fire Chief Retiring, but Staying in Profession," *Florida Times-Union* (Jacksonville, FL), July 28, 2015. http://jacksonville.com.

Chemical companies may also employ firefighters to ensure that their highly volatile products are handled safely and to respond in the event of an accident.

What Training Do They Need?

It is possible to become a firefighter with no more than a high school diploma or a General Education Development (GED) diploma. The GED diploma is issued to high school dropouts who successfully pass the seven-and-a-half-hour GED exam. Firefighters also need to be at least eighteen years old, in good physical condition, drug free, and have a valid driver's license. However, to improve their chances of being hired by city fire departments, prospective firefighters would do well to enroll in training courses before they put in their applications.

Most professional fire departments require their employees to be certified as emergency medical technicians (EMTs). EMTs respond to car crashes and other medical emergencies, performing duties such as restarting hearts that have stopped beating due to trauma, stopping bleeding, and stabilizing patients while they are transported to a nearby hospital. It can take as long as two years to become certified as an EMT. Getting EMT certified before applying to a city fire department will give you an advantage over uncertified applicants, who would likely have to be sent to EMT school by the fire department before they can work in the field.

But even EMT training is not enough to land a job as a firefighter. Many prospective firefighters take community college classes on firefighting techniques to further prepare themselves for employment. These programs enable students to earn associate's degrees. One such program is offered at Southwestern College in Chula Vista, California, which trains firefighters to battle wildfires. Matt Pecos, an instructor in the program, describes some of the training students can expect to undergo: "The full days of hands-on drills are meant to mimic the closest to real-life scenarios on the job."[12] As part of the program, recruits participate in outdoor exercises in which they run up hills carrying heavy gear and learn how to protect themselves from injury.

Once hired, you can expect to undergo training in a fire department's own academy—a process that typically takes three or four months. As a student in the academy, you will learn about that particular department's preferred methods for fighting fires as well as how fires erupt and spread. You will also learn how to properly use equipment and any procedures that are unique to that department.

After completing fire academy, graduates become what are known as apprentice firefighters. After serving their apprenticeships, which typically last four years, they can take a test that is administered by their state and, if they pass, become certified as a professional firefighter.

What Traits Are Important?

As you might expect, firefighters are people who don't shy away from dangerous situations. In fact, danger is something they fully expect to encounter. However, by paying careful attention to details, they learn how to minimize the hazards to themselves and the public. They rely on their training as well as their fellow squad members, and they work as a team to remain safe. They must also be comfortable taking orders and be willing to trust their fellow professionals with their life. "When you're out there, experiencing the fire firsthand, 50 or 100 feet away, there's an adrenalin rush," says Samuel Meade Jr., who fights wildfires in San Carlos, Arizona. "It's coming toward you, and you think, 'What am I doing here?' You think, 'Am I being safe?' That's when you count on your squad leaders, the people on the crew who have more experience. You must trust their judgment."[13]

Much of what firefighters do is physical. In order to excel at the job, they must be able to carry heavy equipment and withstand punishing working conditions—such as intense heat and heavy smoke. They also have to contend with injuries—sometimes serious ones. The International Association of Fire Fighters reports that 40 percent of professional firefighters are injured on the job each year. The most common injuries are those that result from slips and falls, such as muscle sprains and strains.

A Typical Day

Being a firefighter is not a job that takes place during a normal day shift from 9:00 a.m. to 5:00 p.m. In fact, it is more typical for firefighters to work straight through for twenty-four hours and then take the next thirty-six hours off. When they are on duty but not out on a call, firefighters perform routine tasks such as checking the fire company's gear, exercising, conducting fire safety inspections off premises, and cleaning and maintaining the firehouse.

Professionals who fight wildfires have a different typical day. They are usually busiest in the spring through fall, when dry conditions are common. When they go out on calls, they don't end up in buildings or homes but some of the wildest places in the country. "We'll hike for miles or jump in a helicopter that takes us to where the fire is," explains Meade. "Then we cut brush and trees and scrape vegetation and debris." Firefighters who work under these conditions also use different techniques to fight fire. "We're the 'ground pounders,' making a fire line to keep a fire from spreading," explains Meade. "Sometimes we do a 'back-firing,' burning fuel in front of the fire to create a buffer to stop the progression. This is usually done at night when the fire is low intensity."[14]

Salary and Advancement

According to the BLS, in 2015 firefighters earned an average of $46,870 a year. That year there were 327,300 jobs held by firefighters. By the year 2024 another 17,400 paid firefighting jobs are expected to be added, representing average growth when compared with other occupations.

Firefighting jobs are mostly located in big cities. If you live in a suburban community or small town, it is likely that the local fire department is composed of volunteers. Indeed, outfitting and staffing a professional fire department is an expensive undertaking that many small towns and suburban communities cannot afford. Therefore, they must rely on volunteer fire companies that collect donations with which to buy trucks and other equipment and to finance training courses for their members.

As professional firefighters gain experience, they may be able to move up in the ranks. They may move into administrative positions such as battalion chief, district chief, assistant chief, or deputy chief—all jobs that involve supervising other firefighters.

But no matter where firefighters may stand on the career ladder,

Heightened Awareness

"When you go into a room that is pitch black and quiet, other than hearing your own breathing and the breathing of the guy next to you, you listen for the crackle [of the fire]. When you do see it and you hope you see it before you're on it, you go in together, you work together, you get out, and you look differently at each other. I've slowly been able to become a part of that. That is neat."

—Ashlee Vercler, firefighter

Quoted in Mary Schenk, "Urbana Firefighter Didn't Plan on Career," *Champaign (IL) News-Gazette*, October 29, 2014. www.news-gazette.com.

they are all part of something larger than themselves: a group of professionals dedicated to preserving the lives and property of the people in their communities, even as they risk their own lives to do so. Yet the full extent of their sacrifices is not universally known. As former vice president Joe Biden once told a group of firefighters, "You're the single-most underappreciated profession in the world."[15]

Find Out More

Fire & EMS Career Exploring
1325 W. Walnut Hill Ln.
PO Box 152225
Irving, TX 75015
website: www.exploring.org/fire-ems

Fire & EMS Career Exploring is a hands-on program for students up to age twenty who are thinking about a career as a firefighter or EMT. The website contains details about the program, including its cost and how often students meet.

Hotshots
website: www.fs.fed.us/fire/people/hotshots

Hotshots are an elite group of physically fit firefighters who frequently work in remote locations, using equipment they carry with them. Find out information about the US Department of the Interior's Bureau of Land Management's interagency Hotshot Crews, whose duties include putting out wildfires.

International Association of Fire Fighters
1750 New York Ave. NW, Suite 300
Washington, DC 20006
website: http://client.prod.iaff.org

The International Association of Fire Fighters is a labor union that represents about three hundred thousand full-time firefighters. The union lobbies for firefighter safety and proper equipment, among other things. Its website has information on how to become a firefighter and what the job entails.

National Fire Protection Association (NFPA)
1 Batterymarch Park
Quincy, MA 02169-7471
website: www.nfpa.org

This nonprofit organization was established to help save lives and reduce losses from fires that may be caused by faulty electrical wiring and other hazards. Its website has statistics on home fires and reports on firefighter injuries, home fire hazards, and high-rise building fires. You can also read its *NFPA Journal* online.

Nurse-Midwife

A Few Facts

Number of Jobs

About 5,300 as of 2014, expected to grow to 6,600 by 2024

Pay

$96,970, average in 2014

Educational Requirements

Bachelor of science in nursing, plus master's degree from accredited program

Work Settings

Clinics, hospitals, homes

Future Job Outlook

25 percent, much faster than average

A Calling

Nurse-midwives are registered nurses —professionals who have graduated from accredited four-year nursing programs—who have gone on to take advanced training in gynecology and obstetrics. These are the fields of medicine devoted to women's health and childbirth. As nurse-midwives, they are qualified to assist women in childbirth without the oversight of a physician. They belong to a class of nursing professionals known as advanced practice registered nurses (APRNs) and are regarded as being in the top ranks of the nursing field.

Both men and women can become nurse-midwives, although male nurse-midwives are much more rare than female ones. There are some five thousand nurse-midwives in America; of that number, it is believed just about one hundred are men. John Fassett is a certified nurse-midwife in San Francisco. In his thirty-year career, he has assisted in the deliveries of some forty thousand babies. Although he didn't initially set out to be a nurse-midwife, he eventually found himself drawn to the field of obstetrics. "Whether you are called to it and you're a male, or you're called to it and you're a female, it doesn't matter," he says. "You're called to do it."[16]

Those who answer this calling can feel good that the profession is ranked eightieth among the one hundred best jobs, according to U.S. News. The profession receives high marks for its salary, job prospects, and future growth. However, U.S. News notes that the job comes with significant stress and work hours that can be long and unpredictable.

What Nurse-Midwives Do

Pregnant women may choose to see a nurse-midwife instead of an obstetrician—a medical doctor who delivers babies—because they hope to deliver their baby with less medical intervention than they might experience otherwise. They may wish to deliver their baby without drugs, fetal monitors, or routine surgical procedures. Pregnant women who choose the assistance of nurse-midwives can elect to deliver their baby in hospitals, at nurse-midwife clinics, or even at home, if their state allows it. Therefore, nurse-midwives must be prepared to help a mother give birth wherever she chooses. In contrast, few doctors are willing to deliver babies outside of the hospital.

Patients may also elect to use nurse-midwives because they believe those professionals will spend more time with them during their visits. "I'm always moved when I've finished an appointment and hear a woman say, 'No one has ever spent this amount of time discussing issues—or cared enough to make sure I understood—or even waited for me to ask more questions,'"[17] says Ginger Breedlove, president of the American College of Nurse-Midwives.

Nurse-midwives follow their patients throughout their pregnancies, examining them and making sure their baby is developing properly. They educate women on fetal development and what to expect when they give birth. Discussions may involve everything from self-care to infant care, breastfeeding, and family planning. Once a woman is in labor—the process that signals the baby is ready to be born—the nurse-midwife stays with the mother-to-be until the baby has been delivered. Childbirth can take many hours and occur any time of the day or night, making the working hours of attending nurse-midwives—who are always on call—unpredictable.

After they give birth, many women continue to see their nurse-midwives (rather than a physician) for their routine checkups. In fact, many nurse-midwives may serve as their patients' primary medical professional. In fact, many older women continue to see their nurse-midwives when they enter their menopausal years—the time when their bodies are no longer capable of producing eggs. In this way, nurse-midwives may treat their older patients for some of the problems associated with menopause: insomnia, night sweats, pain, and hot flashes, among others. Says Julie Stembridge, a nurse-midwife from Raleigh, North Carolina, "My patients come back for well woman care [and] we continue our partnership in their care. This continuity of care is a very rewarding part of my career."[18]

A Typical Day

No day in the life of a nurse-midwife can be regarded as typical—babies may arrive at 3:00 a.m. or 3:00 p.m. Nevertheless, there are many routine tasks that nurse-midwives carry out as they see their patients. Part of the day may be devoted to examining women in all stages of their pregnancies to ensure they are eating right, taking vitamins, and staying away from alcohol and tobacco—substances that could adversely affect the health of their fetus. Nurse-midwives may look for complications in their patients' pregnancies and, if warranted, refer their patients to physicians. For example, nurse-midwives cannot perform caesarian sections, in which an incision is made to remove the baby, or any other type of surgical procedure.

Part of the day may be devoted to seeing postpartum patients—mothers who have already given birth. These patients will be examined to ensure they are recovering properly from the experience of childbirth, which can be physically taxing. Throughout the day, nurse-midwives may field phone calls from patients who have questions about how their pregnancy is progressing. Stembridge describes her routine work as follows:

> I review a patient's history, perform an exam, order testing and initiate a plan of care. . . . In the hospital, I am responsible for seeing all of the patients from our [practice]. This can include laboring moms, postpartum patients, pregnant patients with complications or postoperative gynecology patients. In the hospital I perform exams, order testing, interpret testing and perform procedures such as ultrasound [and] vaginal delivery.[19]

Moreover, although there is a lot of interaction with patients, nurse-midwives also must deal with paperwork. This includes keeping medical records, writing prescriptions, ordering medical tests, and completing forms for insurance companies.

Is This Career for Me?

You might find the work of a nurse-midwife satisfying if you are a good communicator and problem solver who can stay calm in difficult situations. You should have a genuine empathy for others. Also, students considering careers as nurse-midwives often possess a love of learning—particularly for science. They should be organized and dependable since women count on nurse-midwives to guide them through one of the most challenging and meaningful moments of their life. Nurse-midwives' organizational skills will help them pay attention to whether the baby and mother are progressing according to schedule, keeping appointments, and avoiding complications. Nurse-midwives must also be willing to adjust their schedules at a moment's notice—they must be present to handle emergencies and births no matter when these occur.

Nurse-midwives must also be able to work independently, yet they should know when a situation requires the expertise of another medical professional, such as when a baby needs to be delivered through surgical intervention. Moreover, nurse-midwives must be emotionally sturdy—able to face the sad occasions when births or illnesses result in disability, pain, suffering, and even death.

What Education Is Needed

Nurse-midwife programs are offered through university graduate schools. This means that in order to be admitted to a program, students need to have already earned an undergraduate degree in nursing and passed a test that certifies them as a registered nurse. In addition, some graduate schools require students to have some relevant experience—such as serving as a labor and delivery nurse—before they are admitted.

As undergraduates, student nurses take courses in chemistry, biology, and other sciences. They also receive hands-on experience working with surgical, elderly, pediatric, and mental health patients during their four years of nursing school. While this is the typical path nurse-midwives take, it is also possible to enroll in a nurse-midwife graduate degree program if you have an undergraduate degree in women's studies, psychology, or another non-nursing field. However, students who follow this path will first need to take the nursing courses they lack before they can begin the midwifery portion of their studies. Because of this, their degree as a nurse-midwife will likely take longer to finish.

Students applying to be in upcoming classes of nurse-midwives will find keen competition for a small number of spaces. Graduate school programs limit the number of students they

Available Around the Clock

"I was able to get to know my families and be available for them 24/7. I could follow the women during their pregnancies and take calls day and night, making them feel very supported. Being available to my patients and providing that commitment to them is what kept me in Tomah [Wisconsin] all these years."

—Kathy Kett, nurse-midwife

Quoted in Steve Rundio, "Long-Time Nurse Midwife Retiring from Tomah Gundersen," *La Crosse (WI) Tribune*, June 24, 2016. http://lacrossetribune.com.

admit because educating prospective nurse-midwives requires a lot of hands-on study and mentoring. For that reason, prospective students may be denied admission the first time they apply. Persistence may be required to get a spot in a program.

Among the classes nurse-midwife students take are courses on how to care for women during pregnancy and afterward, as well as newborn care. They can also expect to take classes focused on promoting optimal health outcomes. Students will spend considerable time in clinical settings working with patients under the supervision of instructors. For example, students enrolled in the University of Michigan School of Nursing Nurse-Midwife Program are required to spend at least 730 hours in clinical settings.

After completing school, which usually takes about two years, students need to pass a test to become certified. The American Midwifery Certification Board administers the tests. To maintain their certifications, nurse-midwives need to fulfill certain continuing education requirements or retake the exam every five years.

Where Nurse-Midwives Work

Most nurse-midwives work in doctors' offices and hospitals. Nurse-midwives can also start their own practice if they want. There are other career paths, too. For example, nurse-midwife Deb Erickson-Owens found a job with the US Air Force.

During her time in the military, Erickson-Owens assisted a pregnant woman aboard an air force plane tens of thousands of feet in the sky. Then during a blizzard, she received a ride from a snowplow to arrive at a hospital in time to help the mother of a baby who could not wait until the weather cleared to be born. Erickson-Owens says that given the circumstances, the patient exhibited a lot of courage. "She did it all without drugs," Erickson-Owens says of her patient. "She said to me, 'I've seen a whole side to me that I never knew existed. I'm strong.' And I think those are the pieces that are exciting about being a midwife, you witness women discovering themselves."[20]

Salaries and Future Prospects

As an APRN professional, you could expect to earn about $100,000 or more. Nurse-midwives who work in very populated metropolitan areas earn the highest salaries. The median salary, according to the Bureau of Labor Statistics (BLS), is $96,970 a year. That salary is nearly $30,000 more than what the average registered nurse earns—about $67,500 a year.

Nurse-midwives who practice in California make the most money—particularly those who work in the Los Angeles, San Diego, and San Jose areas. Other cities with outstanding salaries for nurse-midwives are Boston and Dallas.

In addition to above-average salaries, future nurse-midwives can look forward to strong job demand throughout their careers. And while those are certainly terrific inducements, the real satisfactions from this career come from the day-to-day tasks of helping women and their babies achieve opportunities to share healthy lives together.

Find Out More

American College of Nurse-Midwives
8403 Colesville Rd., Suite 1550
Silver Spring, MD 20910
website: www.midwife.org

The mission of the American College of Nurse-Midwives is to support the professional practice of midwifery and midwifery education. The organization certifies nurse-midwives. Its website contains substantial information on how to become a midwife, trends in midwife education, and answers to frequently asked questions about the profession.

American Midwifery Certification Board
849 International Dr., Suite 120
Linthicum, MD 21090
website: www.amcbmidwife.org

The American Midwifery Certification Board oversees standards for the certification of nurse-midwives. Its website has a downloadable candidate handbook and a chart that explains the educational and clinical requirements needed for certification.

Midwives Alliance of North America (MANA)
website: https://mana.org

MANA promotes excellence in midwifery practice, education, and access to quality health care for women, babies, and families. MANA's website has information about the different types of midwives, the legal status of midwives, and the legal status of midwives in individual states.

National Association of Certified Professional Midwives
PO Box 340
Keene, NH 03431
website: http://nacpm.org

A membership organization dedicated to fostering the growth of certified nurse-midwives, the National Association of Certified Professional Midwives has a section for students on how to find a school and become a certified nurse-midwife. Visitors can sign up to receive e-mail news updates about the field and learn about the history of midwifery.

Occupational Therapist

A Few Facts

Number of Jobs

About 114,600 as of 2014, with 30,400 jobs to be added by 2024

Pay

$80,150, average in 2015

Educational Requirements

Master's degree

Work Settings

Schools, hospitals, nursing homes, rehabilitation centers

Future Job outlook

27 percent, much faster than average

Fostering Independence

Occupational therapists (OTs) work with people to help them relearn and perform critical daily functions on their own. Their patients include people who have suffered debilitating accidents as well as those recovering from illness and surgery. Their patients can range in age from young children to the elderly, and many have suffered brain trauma. Although they are physically capable of doing everyday chores on their own, their head injuries have made it necessary to relearn simple functions such as how to turn a key in a lock, wash themselves, or lift a spoon out of a bowl of soup.

The OT complements the role played by a physical therapist in a patient's recovery. A physical therapist's job is to help a patient, say, regain the strength in his or her legs and walk again. The OT works with patients to ensure they can function in their homes and elsewhere as they recover. For example, consider the act of carrying a laundry basket down a flight of stairs. This may seem like an easy task for most people, but it would be challenging for somebody recovering from an accident. Moreover, if done improperly, it could result in a dangerous slip and fall. An OT would therefore work with the patient on ways to maintain balance and stamina as he or she carries a heavy basket of laundry.

Despite what the title might suggest, OTs do not help people find or perform professional occupations. Rather, they focus on helping people take command of the occupations of life. For example, in order to function as a student, you likely have to schedule your time, study, take notes, and carry a backpack. Some students cannot perform these activities without assistance. Perhaps they have autism, a neurological condition that can make it challenging for them to understand social situations and communicate with others. In this situation the OT would work with the autistic student, helping him or her learn to function as normally as possible in school and at home.

Helping people in this way is what got Marvin Reid interested in becoming an OT after he found his job in information technology unrewarding. "After speaking to a friend who worked in occupational

Small Progress Is Exciting

"Sometimes the tiniest baby steps of progress are truly the most exciting. Like the first time a child puts on her sock all by herself. . . . Or the first time parents share with you that they were actually able to take their child to the grocery store or the park or a birthday party without experiencing a meltdown. Or the first time a teacher witnesses a student being able to cut with scissors or sit for and participate in all of circle time instead of running around the room. Progress happens in both the children we work with as well as in the parents and teachers who support them."

—Christie Kiley, an OT

Christie Kiley and Abby Brayton-Chung, "The Most Important Things You Need to Know About Becoming an Occupational Therapy Practitioner: A Guide for Prospective Students," *Mama OT* (blog), 2015. http://mamaot.com.

therapy and listening to her stories of helping improve people's lives, I knew that this was the right path for me,"[21] says Reid. What drew him to the field was the opportunity to help a variety of individuals whose physical problems required them to find new ways to take baths, eat, or perform other tasks to stay independent.

Is This Career for Me?

If being an OT seems like a career you want to pursue, ask yourself if you are comfortable around sick, injured, or disabled persons. Not everyone is. OTs also need to be patient; they may have to repeat lessons for clients multiple times. They must also be prepared for progress to be made slowly, if at all. "You'll need a lot of patience because you'll probably be teaching skills that adults once had but lost due to illness or injury," reports the Princeton Review, an organization that helps students prepare for college admissions and select majors. "You will be helping the muscles to recover or adapt other muscles to do the job, but you'll also be rehabilitating the spirit."[22] Another reason patience is important is because many adults get frustrated when they experience slow progress. It may take them months of working with an OT before they make any progress.

OTs also need to work well on teams. This is because they will likely work very closely with physical therapists, social workers, and physicians. They also need good communication skills, including the ability to write clear and detailed reports that will be read by team members.

How Much Training Does It Take?

To work as an OT, you will need a master's degree in occupational therapy. The fastest way to achieve that goal is to enroll in a five-year OT program that earns you both an undergraduate and master's degree. Getting both degrees separately would take closer to seven years. However, if you majored in something else as an undergraduate—anatomy, biology, or kinesiology (the study of how the body moves), for example—you can still apply to graduate school to get a master's degree in occupational therapy as long as you meet the school's list of prerequisites.

Many universities also require that you spend at least twenty hours shadowing an OT before applying. To get those hours, you will need to contact OTs to see if they are willing to let you observe them as they work. In addition to meeting the entrance requirements, observing OTs can help prospective students get a better feel for the field. "The best way to see if you're suited to occupational therapy is to gain on the ground experience," says Reid. "Classroom training is, of course, valuable but it can only teach you so much. It's not until you're with patients, dealing with real life day-to-day cases, can you really appreciate the job."[23]

Once admitted to an OT program, students spend their days in lectures and classrooms. They also practice working in groups, learning how to evaluate and assess patients' needs. In addition students work with practicing OTs.

Where OTs Work

Patients who need occupational therapy can be found everywhere —in big cities, suburban communities, and small towns. Thus, OTs have many options for where they work. "OTs can find jobs . . . just about anywhere," says Samia Rafeedie, assistant professor of occupational therapy at the University of Southern California–Los Angeles. "It's a ticket to open any doorway."[24]

OTs can find work in schools, hospitals and nursing homes, or private practices that employ OTs and assign them to work in those institutions. Many OTs visit patients in their homes, working with them in their own environments so the patients can learn to overcome the everyday challenges they face. OTs can also be found at some psychiatric facilities, day care centers, military hospitals, and universities, where they conduct research or teach occupational therapy students. No matter what setting they work in, most OTs find their work very satisfying. Says OT Claire Heffron:

> I work in a preschool and primary school building and hardly a day goes by that I don't see the clear and lasting impact of my work on the way my students are able to participate and function in their classrooms and around the school building. From the bus to lunch time to recess to circle time—school-based OTs are able to touch kids' lives in a unique and positive way.[25]

The two biggest employers of OTs are hospitals and professional offices, which together account for about half of all OT jobs, according to the Bureau of Labor Statistics (BLS). Another 12 percent work in schools. Others work in nursing homes and rehabilitation centers or deliver services to people directly in their homes.

Salaries and Future Prospects

The field of occupational therapy is growing, and 30,400 jobs are expected to be added by 2024. Overall, the field has a 27

Late Nights

"On a good day, I get to start going home by 6 p.m. However, on a long day, I might not start going home until 8:30 or 9 p.m. This will depend on whether I work overtime or not, as well as the number of reports I am expected to finish. In some facilities, it can be a lonely feeling when I am the last person to leave on the rehab team. In other facilities, I might be accompanied by some other rehab team members who stay late. After my work is done, I will drive anywhere from 30 minutes to 2 hours home, depending on the distance and traffic."

—Bill Wong, an OT

Quoted in *OT Café*, "A Day in the Life: Skilled Nursing Facility," April 17, 2015. http://abbypediatricot.blogspot.com.

percent growth rate, which is much higher than average. These plus several other factors bode well for those who choose this profession. One is America's aging population, which is growing rapidly as the generation known as the baby boomers gets older. As people age, they are more likely to suffer debilitating diseases such as strokes—which could make them partially paralyzed—or Parkinson's disease, a disorder that impairs physical movement and speech.

However, there is also a need among younger patients for OT. Because of advances in neurological science and general awareness, more young people are being diagnosed with autism. To cope with those rising numbers, more OTs will be needed to work with autistic patients.

Studies have also shown that occupational therapy helps reduce the number of patients that are admitted to hospitals. Of greater importance, however, is that studies indicate that occupational therapy is a significant factor in reducing the number of patients who must be readmitted to hospitals—in other words, patients who receive occupational therapy are less likely to return to a hospital to be retreated because of a relapse suffered at home. For example, a 2016 study published in the health care journal *Medical Care Research and Review* found that OTs have helped patients recovering from heart failure avoid being readmitted to a hospital. One way OTs do this is by working with family members to recognize early signs of trouble in their debilitated loved ones. OTs also assess the patient's home for how well it meets the patient's needs. For example, an OT may recommend that support bars or benches be installed in a shower to reduce the risk of falling. Or the therapist may help the patient learn to use a grabber tool, a device that enables a person to reach an object on a high shelf. Since it is much less expensive for an OT to work with a patient at home than for the patient to be readmitted for a lengthy hospital stay, many hospitals see the value of employing OTs. This need virtually guarantees that growth in the profession will remain robust.

On average, OTs make $80,150 annually, according to the BLS. With the possibility of earning a high salary, perform satisfying work, and plenty of demand for their skills, occupational therapy has much to offer people who are looking for a career that helps others.

Find Out More

American Journal of Occupational Therapy
website: www.aota.org/Publications-News/
AmericanJournalOfOccupationalTherapy.aspx

This academic journal is published by the American Occupational Therapy Association seven times each year. Issues contain articles about the latest research on occupational therapy topics.

American Occupational Therapy Association
website: www.aota.org

The American Occupational Therapy Association is a one-hundred-year-old professional association that represents sixty thousand members across the country. Its website has information on finding a school, the job outlook for OTs, trade publications, advocacy initiatives, and the different types of OT practices that you could work within.

National Board for Certification in Occupational Therapy (NBCOT)
12 S. Summit Ave., Suite 100
Gaithersburg, MD 20877
website: www.nbcot.org

The NBCOT oversees the certification process for OTs and the standards that go along with it. Its website has a short animated video on what occupational therapy is, information on the code of conduct that OTs need to follow, and how to contact state regulatory boards.

OT Café
website: http://abbypediatricot.blogspot.com

This blog was started by a pediatric OT who wanted to create a place to share ideas about occupational therapy. Although it is no longer updated, *OT Café* has many valuable and relevant archived posts about how to choose a college, what to expect in school, and how to evaluate a job offer.

Social Worker

A Few Facts

Number of Jobs

About 649,300 in 2014

Pay

$45,900, average salary in 2015

Educational Requirements

Bachelor's degree

Work Settings

Hospitals, government offices, nursing homes, schools

Future Job Outlook

12 percent, faster than average

Providing a Safety Net

Social workers help people who experience difficulties that may arise from illness, poverty, unemployment, addiction, or disability. They help their clients create plans to address those problems and point them toward resources provided by governments, nonprofit organizations, hospitals, and businesses. For example, before being discharged from a hospital, an elderly man may meet with a social worker to create a plan for his care. The social worker might arrange for visiting nurses to see the patient at his home, make sure his prescriptions are filled, and drop by his house to ensure he is making progress toward recovery.

Social workers don't just work with the elderly; they work with people of all ages. They may help young children living in foster care. Or they may help teens with disabilities find the right schools. They may work with homeless adults, helping them find a job or a permanent place to live. To do their work, social workers need to possess a special blend of skills. "There has to be an ability to respond to people in crisis, to be calm, and to think clearly,"

A social worker meets with an elderly client to discuss his current and future care needs. Social workers assist people of all ages and with a variety of needs; their clients may include elderly individuals, foster youth, couples seeking to adopt children, and teens with disabilities.

says Tracy Whitaker, director of the Center for Workforce Studies at the National Association of Social Workers. "And you have to believe in what you are doing. What's interesting is that most social workers find [the work] very rewarding, and they don't have regrets about choosing social work as a career."[26]

Social work takes a special type of individual—someone who cares deeply about the welfare of others. If you are an empathetic listener, consider yourself resourceful, and are the type of person whose friends seek your advice and help, you already possess many of the traits important to be a successful social worker.

Where Might You Work?

Many schools employ social workers to serve students who have a variety of needs. Some may suffer from abuse at home, others may have psychiatric disorders, and still others may be living in poverty and need help finding food, clothes, and school supplies. State and local government human services agencies often employ many social workers. These agencies include child welfare departments, agencies that meet the needs of older adults, agencies that address addiction, and antipoverty agencies. Because homelessness, poverty, alcoholism, drug abuse, and spousal abuse afflict many Americans across the country, the field of social work is one in which professionals can find many opportunities.

Social workers often find jobs in prisons, where all inmates are assigned a social worker to help them address the problems that led to their incarceration. Social workers also help inmates prepare to lead law-abiding lives when they are released. Aaron Cooper works at Rikers Island, a prison in New York City. He specializes in inmates who suffer from mental illness. "I knew it would be a challenging population," he says. "I kind of wanted to push myself out of my comfort zone."[27]

How Do Social Workers Help Children?

Social workers often work under the title of caseworker. The caseload of a caseworker consists of the clients he or she is assigned to manage. A caseworker who works for a child welfare agency, for example, is typically assigned a caseload of eighteen children, according to the Council of Accreditation, a national organization that recommends standards for human services agencies. The children under the caseworker's care may have been abused by their parents or be the sons or daughters of drug-addicted parents who can no longer care for them. Some of them may have parents who are in prison.

The social worker may arrange for the child to appear in court, where a judge may order the child taken out of the home and placed under the protection of foster parents. Afterward, the social worker stays on the case, ensuring the child receives proper care from foster parents and is given access to other services he or she may need, such as mental health counseling. The social worker may meet with the child in the agency office or go out to see the child, observing him or her at home or in school to ensure the child is experiencing a normal home life and education. "It's not a glamorous job," says Bruce Linder, director of service regions for the Kentucky Cabinet for Health and Family Services. "It's a job where you don't deal in a lot of positives. It takes a special person to do child welfare."[28]

Responding to Emergencies

Social workers must be prepared to respond to emergencies. In the case of a child welfare caseworker, a child might call to report he or she is being abused by a parent. The caseworker is responsible for assessing the danger to the child and responding. The response could include hurrying over to the home to meet with the child and parents. "It can be stressful and seem overwhelming at times," says social worker Karen Green. "Sometimes social workers have to confront people, and I don't enjoy that. For example, I might suggest a child at school is being abused by her

Guided by a Code of Ethics

"In social work, we don't operate on a medical model. Social workers look [at a person's situation] like, 'You've survived this long, and you bring the expertise on your life.'. . . What I love about social work is that there's a code of ethics that requires us to treat clients with dignity and respect, meet them where they are, and not have all the answers."

—Kim White, social worker

Quoted in Jean Tarbett Hardiman, "Career in Social Work Has Led Woman to Advocacy," AP Regional State Report–West Virginia, August 13, 2016.

parent. But I just can't come right out and say to the parent, 'You are this child's problem and this is what you need to do.' I have to find a more tactful way to get my message across."[29]

As most social workers know, calls from troubled clients can come at any hour on any day. Social workers know they may be called on nights and weekends, and they accept that unusual hours are part of the job. In fact, many human services agencies schedule staff members to work nights and weekends, as this is often when clients need their help.

At the Los Angeles County Department of Children and Family Services, for example, social workers typically receive the most calls relating to child abuse cases on Friday and Saturday nights. These are idle times that can often turn dangerous for children. "A typical Friday night could be anywhere from 40 to 55 child abuse investigations for my staff," says Javier Avila, a supervisor in the Los Angeles office. "[These] can include child accidents, child fatalities, near drownings, or near fatalities. So we pretty much get the very severe types of cases on Friday and Saturday nights."[30]

How Much Education Do You Need?

To find a job as a caseworker, you need to have at least a bachelor's degree in social work or a related field such as psychology or sociology. To advance in the profession, you would do well to earn a master's degree. In fact, according to the National Association of Social Workers, only about 12 percent of social workers have a bachelor's degree, while virtually all others have gone on to earn master's degrees.

With a master's degree plus two years' experience as a caseworker, you can qualify for a position as a clinical social worker. These professionals often perform many of the same functions as caseworkers, but their work primarily focuses on clients who suffer from mental illness and might need psychiatric counseling. For example, a client who suffers from schizophrenia—a disorder that affects one's ability to act rationally—would need a different type of counseling than a client who is deeply depressed and potentially suicidal. Therefore, clinical social workers need to become experts in mental illness and work closely with clients to ensure they are receiving proper care. They may be called on to provide an initial diagnosis of a client's mental illness and offer a degree of counseling.

The fastest way to become a social worker is to enroll in a combined bachelor's and master's degree program that takes five years to complete. As a master's degree student, you would study the concepts behind psychiatric therapy, perform research, and gain experience in real work environments.

Salaries and Job Growth

Social workers' salaries vary widely, depending on how they are employed. In 2015 the Bureau of Labor Statistics (BLS) reported that the average annual wage for a social worker employed by a hospital was $56,650 per year. Salaries for other social workers include those who work for government agencies ($46,940), nursing homes ($40,440), and nonprofit agencies ($38,760). The BLS does not provide statistics for the position of clinical social worker, but in 2015 the website PayScale reported that clinical social workers generally earned higher salaries than caseworkers; for example, clinical social workers with at least five years' experience earned as much as $70,520 per year. For these and other reasons, U.S. News placed the position of clinical social worker sixty-second on its list of the one hundred best jobs in 2015.

The field of social work is poised to benefit from better-than-average job growth. The BLS projects that opportunities in social work will increase 12 percent through 2024—a pace well above average. As for specific types of social work, jobs for those in health care, mental health, and substance abuse are forecast to experience a 19 percent growth rate through 2024. Jobs for child, family, and school social workers will grow at a slower rate of 6 percent.

In all, the field is expected to add 74,800 jobs by 2024. Society will need social workers to address the increasing numbers of elderly citizens whose health and financial needs require them to seek relief from social safety networks. Also, many state and county governments want to reduce prison costs by finding alternative treatments for some criminals, and it is anticipated that social workers will be needed to address the mentally ill and addicted clients who would otherwise be jailed. Finally, many Americans continue to live in poverty. This means that social workers will be needed to address problems such as unemployment, hunger, and the care of children. No matter what area of social work you choose, there is little doubt that your work will make someone's life better than it was before.

Find Out More

Council on Social Work Education
website: www.cswe.org

The Council on Social Work Education accredits social work education programs in the United States. It links educational and professional institutions, individual practitioners, and students. The website has a section for students about scholarships, internship opportunities, and accreditation.

Human Services

website: www.humanservicesedu.org/lcswvsmsw.html

Human Services is a website that provides information about careers that give back to communities. The site discusses careers in social work, education and licensing, and where to find schools near you. It also lists human services agencies and provides answers to frequently asked questions.

National Association of Social Workers

750 First St. NE, Suite 800
Washington, DC 20002
website: www.socialworkers.org

Representing 132,000 members, the National Association of Social Workers is the world's largest professional organization for social workers. Its website has a career center with job postings, articles on social work topics, advocacy information, and information for those who wish to learn more about social work.

O*Net OnLine

website: www.onetcenter.org

This free occupational information database is sponsored by the US Department of Labor's Employment and Training Administration. Users can search it for specific information on child, family, and school social workers; health care social workers; and mental health and substance abuse social workers.

Speech-Language Pathologist

Speech Therapy Providers

A speech-language pathologist—also known as a speech therapist—helps people deal with disorders that affect the way they speak. Because of the nature of some speech disorders, a speech-language pathologist may also help people improve their ability to swallow, breathe, and even think.

Speech-language therapists can be found in some surprising places and some traditional ones. For example, it is likely that there is a speech-language pathologist on staff at your school. This professional works with students to address issues such as stuttering; dysarthria, which is speech that is slow, mumbled, or slurred; and childhood apraxia, which is the inability of the brain to form sounds, syllables, or words.

Left untreated, the lack of good verbal skills can lead to lives of isolation and dependence on others. Speech therapists can work to avoid this. Maricor Pagsanjan, a speech-language pathologist at the Bridge School, a school for young people with speech and physical impairments in Hillsborough, California, says:

Our lives revolve [around] communicating with the outside world, and if we want the clients to be able to integrate into society, they need to communicate accurately and effortlessly. . . . I work with teenagers, and I take them out to cafes or bookstores to help them see what communication can do for them. . . . We have to teach our clients that they will have the independence of conducting their lives with communication.[31]

Adults may also need speech therapy—even ones who have been well spoken their whole lives. Sometimes, older adults may suffer a stroke, a condition in which blood is temporarily cut off from the brain. This can cause aphasia, a neurological disorder that disrupts one's ability to speak. To regain the power of speech, these patients may need the services of speech-language pathologists.

What Skills Do You Need?

Speech-language pathologists need to possess some well-developed skills to perform their complicated jobs. First, they need to be good listeners so they can diagnose and treat their clients' needs and issues. They also need sharp analytical skills to decide what tests to order and interpret the results. Then they need to use the results to develop treatment plans for their clients and update those plans as their clients progress through therapy.

Speech-language pathologists also need to be skilled communicators themselves, since part of their job is to relate test results and treatment plans to their clients and family members or other caregivers. This information needs to be relayed in nontechnical terms, in language clients find easy to understand.

Above all, though, speech-language pathologists need to be empathetic and encouraging. "There's . . . a very important counseling component to our profession," says Laurie Sterling, a speech-language therapist at Methodist Hospital in Houston, Texas. "We counsel patients and their families and deal with heartaches and tears because of the limitations and challenges our patients face. It's a unique combination of science, compassion and art."[32]

How to Become a Speech-Language Pathologist

Speech-language pathologists need to possess an undergraduate degree from a four-year university and a master's degree from a program accredited by the Council on Academic Accreditation in Audiology and Speech-Language Pathology. There are more than three hundred such programs at American universities.

Most people who apply to graduate school on this career track have already earned an undergraduate degree in communication science and disorders. Therefore, they already have a foundation in how to treat speech, hearing, and language development problems. Students who majored in other fields would need to take prerequisite courses before they can be considered for a graduate school program. Such courses may include anatomy and physiology, statistics, educational psychology, and language development.

Prospective students should know that graduate schools are very selective in whom they accept. Speech-language pathology training requires students to be mentored by professionals in the field, and one-on-one. Therefore, graduate school enrollment is often limited to the number of mentors who are available to students. This means that graduate school programs are highly selective. For example, the speech-language pathology

Controlling Stuttering

"Austin has made great progress, but I purposely try and make it hard for him in therapy so that we can practice techniques for controlling his stuttering. I want him to stutter when he's here so I can work with him on techniques to use when it happens at school or at home."

—Shelly Vaughn, speech-language pathologist

Quoted in Akron Children's Hospital, "A Day in the Life of a Speech-Language Pathologist," October 21, 2014. https://inside.akronchildrens.org.

program at the University of Maryland–College Park can accommodate twenty-five students per year—but usually gets ten times as many applicants. Students who want to pursue a career as a speech-language pathologist would thus do well to apply to multiple schools to enhance their chance of getting admitted.

After graduation, the prospective speech-language pathologist needs to become certified. Most states require speech-language pathologists to be certified by the American Speech-Language-Hearing Association (ASHA). Becoming certified means passing the organization's exam and two other hurdles—working at least four hundred hours in a clinical setting and completing a nine-month fellowship under the guidance of a certified speech-language pathologist.

How They Do Their Jobs

Speech-language pathologists work at schools and in private practices, where they collaborate with physical therapists and occupational therapists. Hospitals, nursing homes, and other residential care facilities also employ speech-language pathologists.

Speech-language pathologist Shelly Vaughn works on the staff of Akron Children's Hospital in Ohio. Her clients are young patients who, for a variety of reasons, have difficulty speaking. She says:

> Once children start expressing themselves, we sometimes see that they have difficulty making sounds that allow them to be understood. I have to teach some patients how to coordinate all the muscles necessary to make a sound— connecting the brain to the mouth and then making the sound happen. It's a complex process to learn communication skills, and we are here to help kids anywhere there is a breakdown in the development of that process.[33]

One of Vaughn's clients is an eighth-grade student named Austin who has stuttered his whole life. Vaughn teaches Austin mental techniques such as slowing down his rate of speech, learning how to coordinate his breathing and speaking, and thinking of what to say before attempting to utter his words. She also teaches him physical techniques, such as how to relax his mouth and to use his lips, tongue, teeth, and roof of his mouth to form sounds. As Austin practices articulating sentences, he occasionally stutters. When that happens, Vaughn makes him restart his sentence. "Rather than allowing him to push through his blocks and repetitions, I want him to become more aware of when they are happening,"[34] she says.

Job Growth and Salary

According to the Bureau of Labor Statistics (BLS), the profession of speech-language pathology is growing at 21 percent, and about 28,900 positions are expected to be added through 2024. BLS statistics indicate that in 2015, speech-language pathologists earned average salaries of $73,410 per year—an amount that makes the profession attractive to students who have put in many years of education and clinical training to become certified.

In part, growth in the field is expected to be driven by the number of aging baby boomers—people born from 1945 through 1964. As they get older, this large population will require a lot of health services, including those of speech-language pathologists, who may help them with tasks such as recovering the ability to swallow and form words after suffering a stroke or another medical emergency. In addition, many speech pathologists who are baby boomers themselves are retiring, leaving job openings that will be filled by younger people.

Of course, aging baby boomers are but one reason the future for speech-language pathologists looks so promising. ASHA has identified other reasons, too. For instance, as medical interventions improve, more and more people are surviving serious accidents and illnesses that in the past may have killed them. Among these will be survivors of strokes, accidents, and diseases such as cancer. This growing population represents a larger pool who might benefit from speech therapy services.

Taking Work Home

"Speech pathologists get into their field because they want to help people. Unfortunately, the time spent in meetings and doing paperwork can interfere with their ability to actually do their job. Hence why so many SLPs [speech-language pathologists] take work home. There are not enough hours in the day to do all that is expected of them in many settings. It is common for SLPs to sacrifice their personal time so that their students still get their services."

—Katie Yeh, speech-language pathologist

Katie Yeh, "The 10 Biggest Challenges of Being a Speech Pathologist," Friendship Circle Organization, March 3, 2014. www.friendshipcircle.org.

Meeting the needs of children will also be a fruitful area of practice. The US government requires all children to receive an education, including those with special needs. As more children are tested and diagnosed earlier for interventions, there will be a greater need for the services of speech-language pathologists.

Meanwhile, as hospitals, schools, nursing homes, and other live-in health facilities try to reduce their costs of caring for patients, demand for speech-language pathologists' services in private practices is expected to rise. Hospitals have found it less expensive to pay for the services of speech-language professionals than to employ them full-time on staff. Therefore, speech-language therapists in private practice may serve clients at numerous hospitals.

Students who are looking for a demanding career in a helping profession and are willing to go to graduate school and complete certification requirements are likely to find a satisfying future as a speech-language pathologist. Not only will they be well compensated, but they will also enjoy varied duties and the opportunity to serve people of all ages.

Find Out More

American Speech-Language-Hearing Association (ASHA)
website: www.asha.org

ASHA is the professional and credentialing association for speech-language pathologists and related professionals. Its website has a career center with information on undergraduate and graduate degree programs, including the number of students admitted, their grade point averages, and typical test scores. There is also a short video on the future of speech-language pathology (and audiology).

Autism Speaks
website: www.autismspeaks.org

Autism Speaks is a website devoted to imparting information about autism, including what its symptoms are, research being done on the condition, and therapies that can be impactful, such as speech therapy.

Council on Academic Accreditation in Audiology and Speech-Language Pathology (CAA)
American Speech-Language-Hearing Association
2200 Research Blvd., #310
Rockville, MD 20850
website: http://caa.asha.org

The CAA is the accrediting body of ASHA, establishing standards for master's degree and doctoral programs in speech-language therapy. The CAA website has resources for students that include a video on the value of choosing a CAA-accredited program and a warning for prospective students about diploma and accreditation mills that provide dubious credentials that are likely to waste students' money.

SLPJobs
website: www.slpjobs.com

This online career center lists resources for those seeking jobs as speech therapists and resources for people interested in the profession. Students can read articles about finding a job in the field and access a list of state speech-language pathology associations with their contact information.

Special Education Teacher

A Few Facts

Number of Jobs

About 450,700 in 2014

Pay

$56,800, average salary in 2015

Educational Requirements

Bachelor's degree

Work Settings

Public, private, and charter schools

Future Job Outlook

6 percent, about average

Educating People with Disabilities

Special education teachers help students who have emotional, physical, or mental deficits make lives for themselves in society. Government regulations require that every student capable of benefiting from special education must have his or her needs met. This is accomplished through individualized plans that are created by special education teachers and shared with school administrators and parents. Plans vary widely from student to student and are regularly updated to ensure goals are met.

Under their plan, students may receive extra help with reading, math, and writing. Students with visual or hearing impairments typically receive different assistance than those who use wheelchairs or suffer from a learning disability such as dyslexia (which makes it difficult to read) or dyscalculia (which interferes with one's ability to do simple math calculations). "Special ed teachers (are) like the firefighters, marines and special forces of education," says Michael Humphrey, chair of the Special Education Department at

Boise State University in Idaho. "They need to teach the hard to reach and difficult to teach."[35]

Special education teachers are assigned a fixed number of students. Some special needs students are taught in their own separate classes, while others are integrated into the same classes as non–special needs students. Part of the job involves encouraging students to see themselves as achievers and contributing members of society while countering their natural tendency to think of themselves as outsiders. Meghan Mathis, a special education teacher in Bridgewater, New Jersey, says:

> All of us love that a-ha moment when a student's world expands just a little bit because of something we have taught them. . . . I have found that those moments are even more phenomenal because, sadly, often the students are not sure they are capable of learning. When you help a student who thinks they can't learn to achieve things far beyond what they ever dreamed possible—you feel like you can fly.[36]

Who Makes a Good Special Education Teacher?

Special education teachers have to be adept at working with students who can sometimes be challenging. They must also work well with parents, school administrators, and other teachers whose teaching styles may be different from their own. Therefore, special education teachers need to work well with others. Moreover, they need to be resourceful, patient, and able to cope with their own frustrations as well as those of their students. "There are so many things to get you riled up!" says Lisa Parnello, a special education teacher in Santa Clara, California. "Endless meetings, kids who still don't understand a concept after you've taught it 6 different (thoughtful) ways, the kid who enters your room screaming and doesn't stop for 30 minutes thanks to something completely out of your control . . . the list goes on. . . . If you lose it, the kids do, too!"[37]

Small Steps

"My kids have changed my life more than I ever thought anyone could. It's a very challenging profession but the reward outweighs the challenges. You get to see kids develop in slow motion. You get to appreciate and praise the small steps in developments."

—Alyssa Tyson, special education teacher

Quoted in Nika Anschuetz, "Special Education Teacher Shortage Creates Opportunity for Students," *USA Today*, December 14, 2015. http://college.usatoday.com.

What Training Is Necessary?

Special education teachers take the same classes as other teachers and then undergo additional training to become certified to teach students who are disabled or developmentally delayed. Having this extra certification can make a special education teacher more employable than a regular classroom teacher. "A special education certification makes you more hirable than an elementary certificate alone," says Mathis. "With school districts all over the country facing growing budget deficits, anything you can do to be more attractive to the school districts you are applying to is a smart idea."[38]

While in college, students who major in special education learn the basics they need to join the field. They typically graduate with an understanding of educational psychology, technology that can benefit nonverbal and other special needs students, and instructional planning. They will also be required to do student teaching in real classrooms.

Christina Cole graduated from college in 2014 with a degree in special education. During her last semester in college, she student taught sixth-grade special education students. Her experience teaching math and language arts was challenging. "My internship was stressful, demanding, and an emotional roller coaster; on the other hand, it was enjoyable, rewarding, and awe-inspiring," she says. "I learned a great deal in a short amount of time and discovered my life's passion."[39]

After graduation, and depending on the states where they work, special education teachers will need to earn certifications in order to be hired. To obtain these, they will need to undergo background checks, which ensure they do not have a criminal record. They are also required to pass certification tests that are administered by their state.

Where Do Special Education Teachers Work?

Most public school districts employ special education teachers, assigning them to students in elementary, middle, and high schools. Special education teachers also work in private schools. In most public and private schools, the size of the special education staff depends largely on the size of the school and the school's population of special needs students. Therefore, a small elementary school in a rural school district would likely have just

Having a Mission Is Important

"A clear understanding of your core values is critical when embarking on a special education teaching career. You will teach alongside many colleagues each day—some who share your teaching philosophy and some who do not. But it's all about what you can do for your students and how you can guide them to become self-advocates. This sense of values, this mission, becomes your focused strength. When your core values are set, you grow personally and professionally. And your values will evolve as you evolve."

—Elizabeth Stein, special education teacher

Elizabeth Stein, "Teaching Secrets: Advice for a New Special Ed. Teacher," *Education Week*, June 30, 2010. www.edweek.org.

a single special education teacher on staff—or even one teacher who serves two or more schools.

Large, urban schools typically employ an entire staff of special education teachers. Some private schools are devoted entirely to special needs students and therefore also employ many such teachers. For example, the Devereux Glenholme School, a private boarding school in Washington, Connecticut, has a student body composed of young people who suffer from a number of mental health disorders, including depression, autism, and attention-deficit/hyperactivity disorder. The school maintains an enrollment of about eighty students and provides a four-to-one faculty-to-student ratio, meaning there are at least twenty special education teachers on staff. Other private schools that serve special education students maintain similar faculty-to-student ratios.

A Typical Day

At the most basic level, a special education teacher's job is no different from that of a regular classroom teacher: They help their students learn by providing them with knowledge. Of course, special education teachers face challenges not found in typical classrooms. They may find themselves teaching students who have very short attention spans, for example. In such cases they must constantly find ways to keep their students focused on their work.

Moreover, they must learn the nuances and needs of every student. Parnello says one of her former students often threw fits during writing lessons. At first, Parnello thought her student had an aversion to writing, but she concluded he was actually hungry—writing lessons occurred right before lunch. The student was simply expressing his frustration with being hungry. "His fast metabolism made him need to eat sooner," she says. "I made the rule 'A bite and a write' which meant he had to take a bite and write while he chews."[40] Parnello concluded that the boy's behavior was hunger related by keeping a journal.

In addition to interpreting students' behavior patterns, special education teachers have to prepare themselves for unexpected messes. For example, special education teacher Tim Villegas says he learned early in his career to always keep a change of clothes in his locker. "You never know what kind of fluid or edible material you might find flying around,"[41] he says.

Salary and Working Conditions

According to the Bureau of Labor Statistics (BLS), special education teachers who work in high schools earn the highest salaries in the profession; in 2015 they averaged $58,500 per year. Meanwhile, middle school special education teachers earn average salaries of $57,280, while those in elementary schools and kindergartens earn $55,810 a year. Finally, special education teachers who work in preschools earn average salaries of $53,990 a year.

Most special education teachers work in classrooms. They typically start their workday before students arrive and end them hours after the students have left. They sometimes do work at home, grading papers, making lessons plans, and filling out other paperwork. As most school districts work on a ten-month schedule, the typical special education teacher has the summer off to relax, take continuing education courses, or work a summer job.

Future Outlook

There are currently about 450,700 special education teachers in the United States. According to the BLS, employment in this profession is expected to increase at a rate of 6 percent through 2024. By then about twenty-eight thousand new jobs are expected to be created in the field. While this job growth rate is considered average, there will always be places for special education teachers in school districts, private schools, and residential facilities. Moreover, new teachers may benefit from a countrywide shortage of special education teachers needed to replace ones who retire.

Job seekers who are willing to teach in rural areas will probably have the easiest time getting their first position. "There's a desperate need for highly trained and highly qualified special education teachers in the work force,"[42] says Brian Uplinger, superintendent of Central Greene School District, a rural public school district in Greene County, Pennsylvania. Uplinger says his school district constantly finds it challenging to get recent college graduates who have special education certifications to teach in the district's rural schools. It has been particularly hard to find special education teachers who are certified to teach math to special needs students.

Once hired, there is room for advancement. As they gain experience, teachers can move into leadership positions in their school's special education department. They may supervise or mentor new teachers and student teachers. However, whether they supervise other teachers or stay in the classroom, they will make a difference in the lives of numerous students.

Find Out More

Council for Exceptional Children
2900 Crystal Dr., Suite 1000
Arlington, VA 22202-3557
website: www.cec.sped.org

The Council for Exceptional Children is a professional association of educators dedicated to advancing the success of special needs and gifted children. It accomplishes its mission through advocacy, standards, and professional development.

Education World
75 Mill Rd.
Colchester, CT 06415
website: www.educationworld.com

This award-winning online resource for teachers offers education news, lesson plans by subject and age, and professional development articles. Education World has a section devoted to topics of interest to special education teachers.

National Association of Special Education Teachers
1250 Connecticut Ave. NW, Suite 200
Washington, DC 20036
website: www.naset.org

The National Association of Special Education Teachers exists to promote the professionalism of special education teachers across the country and to prepare people to enter the field. Its website has news about special education issues, career advice for teachers, and job postings along with the requirements you would need to apply for them.

Personnel Improvement Center
National Association of State Directors of Special Education
1800 Diagonal Rd., Suite 320
Alexandria, VA 22314
website: www.personnelcenter.org

Originally created with funding from the federal government, the Personnel Improvement Center is dedicated to recruiting, preparing, and retaining special education teachers and early intervention specialists. Its website offers guidance on how to become a special education teacher, a means to explore careers in special education, and information on obtaining certification.

SOURCE NOTES

Introduction: Making a Difference

1. Quoted in George James, "Teaching Adults to Read," *New York Times*, January 18, 1998. www.nytimes.com.
2. Quoted in University of Chicago, "Looking for Satisfaction and Happiness in a Career? Start by Choosing a Job That Helps Others," April 17, 2007. www.news.uchicago.edu.
3. Jessica Amortegui, "Finding Meaning at Work Is More Important Than Being Happy," *FastCompany.com*, June 26, 2014. www.fastcompany.com.
4. Quoted in Paul Froese, *On Purpose: How We Create the Meaning of Life*. New York: Oxford University Press, 2016, pp. 21–22.

Addiction Counselor

5. Quoted in Careers in Psychology, "Donna Mae Depola: Substance Abuse Counselor." http://careersinpsychology.org.
6. Quoted in *U.S. News & World Report*, "Substance Abuse and Behavioral Disorder Counselor: Reviews & Advice," 2017. http://money.usnews.com.
7. Rita Sommers-Flanagan and John Sommers-Flanagan, *Becoming an Ethical Helping Professional*. Hoboken, NJ: Wiley, 2015, p. 168.
8. Quoted in Careers in Psychology, "Donna Mae Depola."

Adult Literacy Teacher

9. Quoted in Kimberly Reynolds, "6 Reasons Why Teaching ESL Is a Rewarding Career Choice," My English Teacher, June 6, 2012. www.myenglishteacher.eu.
10. Quoted in Literary Information and Communication System, "Teacher Effectiveness in Adult Education—Full Transcript—Adult Literacy Professional Development Discussion List," May 10, 2012. https://lincs.ed.gov.

Firefighter

11. Quoted in Jessica Flores, "Firefighter Captured in Viral Photo Speaks Out," Fox 10 Phoenix, December 23, 2015. www.fox10phoenix.com.
12. Quoted in Lisa Cox, "San Diego NWR: Fire Crew Assists with Local College Fire Academy for Ninth Year," US Fish & Wildlife Service, April 5, 2014. www.fws.gov.

13. Quoted in Elka Torpey, "Interview with a Firefighter," Bureau of Labor Statistics, June 2015. www.bls.gov.
14. Quoted in Torpey, "Interview with a Firefighter."
15. Quoted in Julie Shaw, "Biden Honors Two Fallen Firefighters," *Philadelphia Inquirer*, October 2, 2016, p. B8.

Nurse-Midwife

16. Quoted in Hoodline, "'Boys Just Don't Do That': Meet the Castro's Pioneering Male Nurse Midwife," September 27, 2016. http://hoodline.com.
17. Quoted in *U.S. News & World Report*, "Nurse-Midwife Overview," 2016. http://money.usnews.com.
18. Quoted in Kaitlin Louie, "Interview with Julie Stembridge, MSN, CNM-Certified Nurse Midwife," Online FNP Programs, 2016. www.onlinefnpprograms.com.
19. Quoted in Louie, "Interview with Julie Stembridge, MSN, CNM-Certified Nurse Midwife."
20. Quoted in Kaitlyn Murray, "Rhode Island's Top Nurses 2016," *Rhode Island Monthly*, September 2016. www.rimonthly.com.

Occupational Therapist

21. Marvin Reid, "Occupational Therapy: 'Why I Swapped a Job in IT for a Career Helping Others,'" *Guardian* (Manchester), July 23, 2014. www.theguardian.com.
22. Princeton Review, "Occupational Therapy," 2017. www.princetonreview.com.
23. Reid, "Occupational Therapy: 'Why I Swapped a Job in IT for a Career Helping Others.'"
24. Quoted in *U.S. News & World Report*, "Occupational Therapist Reviews & Advice," 2016. http://money.usnews.com.
25. Claire Heffron, "A Day in the Life of a School-Based OT, Part 1," *OT Café* (blog), April 20, 2015. http://abbypediatricot.blogspot.com.

Social Worker

26. Quoted in Charlotte Huff, "Hope to Help," *Career World*, April–May 2010, p. 18.
27. Aaron Cooper, Jennifer Perez, and Paul Felker, "Here's a Window in the Days of Three Social Workers," *Career World*, April–May 2010, p. 19.
28. Quoted in Claire Galofaro, "Social Worker Turnover Leads to High Caseloads," *Louisville (KY) Courier-Journal*, February 6, 2015. www.courier-journal.com.

29. Quoted in Libby Jacobson, "The Caring Career," *New Moon*, July–August 2006, p. 20.
30. Quoted in KPCC Radio, "Friday Nights Bring the Toughest Cases for DCFS Social Workers," November 15, 2013. www.scpr.org.

Speech-Language Pathologist

31. Maricor Pagsanjan, "Speech Therapy: Communicating with Fun and Purpose," SpeechTherapist.com, August 2, 2016. http://speechtherapist.com.
32. Quoted in Cynthia Stephens, "Speech Pathology Combines 'Science, Compassion and Art,'" *Houston Chronicle*, November 5, 2012. www.chron.com.
33. Quoted in Akron Children's Hospital, "A Day in the Life of a Speech-Language Pathologist," October 21, 2014. https://inside.akronchildrens.org.
34. Quoted in Akron Children's Hospital, "A Day in the Life of a Speech-Language Pathologist."

Special Education Teacher

35. Quoted in Nika Anschuetz, "Special Education Teacher Shortage Creates Opportunity for Students," *USA Today*, December 14, 2015. http://college.usatoday.com.
36. Meghan Mathis, "5 Things I Wish I Had Known Before I Became a Special Education Teacher," TeachHUB. www.teachhub.com.
37. Lisa Parnello, "Tips for New Special Education Teachers," *A Special Sparkle* (blog), July 7, 2013. www.aspecialsparkle.com.
38. Mathis, "5 Things I Wish I Had Known Before I Became a Special Education Teacher."
39. Christina Cole, "Five Tips for Surviving Student Teaching in Special Education," Special Education Guide, January 12, 2015. www.specialeducationguide.com.
40. Parnello, "Tips for New Special Education Teachers."
41. Tim Villegas, "Things I Wish I Knew My First Year of Teaching Special Education," Think Inclusive, February 18, 2016. www.thinkinclusive.us.
42. Quoted in Anschuetz, "Special Education Teacher Shortage Creates Opportunity for Students."

Carmen Altopiedi is a medical case manager at a nonprofit community health center in Pennsylvania that provides primary care, consumer education, research, and advocacy, primarily for the HIV/AIDS population. A licensed social worker and licensed clinical social worker, he helps clients obtain health insurance, housing, and drug and alcohol services. He also supervises other social workers on staff.

Q: Why did you become a social worker?

A: I went back to school at thirty-seven after working for twenty years in the food and beverage industry. I knew I wanted a change but initially returned to school without knowing what career I wanted; I just knew I wanted to finish my bachelor's degree. I started taking some social work classes and found them interesting. I enjoyed the people I met in that field and some of the grassroots work they were doing. From there I just decided I would go on to my master's in social work at Rutgers-Camden (in New Jersey).

Q: Can you describe your typical workday?

A: I come in around 9 a.m. and spend the first half hour or so listening to voicemails that came in since I last checked. Of course, I have scheduled clients I have to see but must also work with clients without appointments who come to the office with emergencies. My day is also filled with administrative work or filling out paperwork. Also, as part of my job, I provide clinical supervision for six other social workers, who are working on obtaining their clinical licenses. My day usually ends around 5 p.m.

Q: What do you like most about your work?

A: I really enjoy interacting with people. That's why I tell people that going from the food and beverage industry into social work was a lateral move; I worked with people then, and I work with people now, using many of the same skills. Of course, my current clients' needs are very different than those patronizing a restaurant. I most enjoy interacting with people—and interacting with my colleagues.

Q: What do you like least about your work?

A: My least favorite part of the job is the paperwork. There is a lot of it and it does take up a large chunk of my time, perhaps as much as 20 percent.

Q: What personal qualities do you find most valuable for being a social worker?

A: You have to be empathetic. You also have to have the desire to be a change-agent to help people, and to kind of walk in their shoes, attempting to understand their feelings and road blocks that make change so difficult. You act as a navigator to help people find their way without actually doing the work for them. Being flexible, caring, and having the ability to listen and give positive feedback are essential.

Q: What advice do you have for students who might be interested in this career?

A: You have to have a strong desire to work with people and you have to have a lot of patience and motivation, knowing that, perhaps, in the beginning, you will not be making a lot of money. If your ambition is financial, then this is the wrong career for you. Not that you can't make a lot of money if you focus on the administrative side of social work.

Q: Is there anything you wish you had known before choosing this career?

A: There are on-going tests and clinical courses that you need to take throughout your career to keep up your license. You have to be prepared to take state boards [exams] and to keep taking courses to keep your licensure current. This can be costly and time-consuming but adds to the legitimacy of the career.

OTHER CAREERS IF YOU LIKE HELPING PEOPLE

Clergy
Dance therapist
Dentist
Doctor
Doula
Financial advisor
Home health aide
Hospital orderly
Legal assistant
Librarian
Life coach
Mental health counselor
Music therapist
Nutritionist
Paramedic
Pharmacist
Physical therapist

Police officer
Psychologist
Public defender
Realtor
Rehabilitation counselor
Reporter
School counselor
Social and human service
    assistant
Soldier
State representative
Substitute teacher
Translator
Veterinarian
Veterinary assistant
Wedding planner
Youth director

Editor's note: The online *Occupational Outlook Handbook* of the US Department of Labor's Bureau of Labor Statistics is an excellent source of information on jobs in hundreds of career fields, including many of those listed here. The *Occupational Outlook Handbook* may be accessed online at www.bls.gov/ooh.

INDEX

ABOUT THE AUTHOR

Gail Snyder is a freelance writer and advertising copywriter who has written more than twenty-five books for young readers. She has a degree in journalism from Pennsylvania State University and lives in Chalfont, Pennsylvania, with her husband, Hal Marcovitz.